EVERYTHING
YOU NEED TO START YOUR OWN CLEANING BUSINESS

and how to make it successful with sales

EVERYTHING
YOU NEED TO START YOUR OWN CLEANING BUSINESS

and how to make it successful with sales

SHANAYA PEARSON

CONTENTS

PROLOGUE

I first started my cleaning company on June 12, 2020. At the time, I was cleaning residential and commercial properties. Before that it was my mother, Melissa Yvette Pearson, who introduced me to this business. She was cleaning homes and worked for a hospital until her diabetes forced her to stop. I learned a lot from her and she was the one who gave me my skill in this industry. From the beginning I knew that I wanted the business to grow and have employees working with me. I read as much as I could and even studied a YouTube channel called Angela Brown before I started the business. Soon I signed up for c-corporation and named business Catrese Special Services Inc.

In this company we offer High Quality Cleaning Services. I know you may be wondering why I say high quality, well that is because we are an unique cleaning company. If you are reading this, that is something you may want to consider for your business. You always want to stand out from the rest because you will have a lot of competition out there in this industry.

When I first started my prices was very low but I wanted to get my name out there and get as much business as I could. At the time, my prices were $25 per hour for each cleaning. I had over ten clients and customers. I paid for a $25 flyer from my designer. His name is Max Remy (305) 509-9024 and he does amazing work so I highly recommend him. I posted in over ten facebook free business groups as well as regular groups. This was the beginning of my network marketing. My main goal was to discover and reach my targeted audience.

At first it was realtors who needed move in cleanings, every week, biweekly consistent clients that wanted their home cleaned frequently. I was very new to all of this but I tried my best in the beginning stages of running my business. There was a lot of learning to do and I got few complaints about my cleaning. It took time but I remained focused and have come a long way.

I started my company June 12, 2020, now it's 2024. It has been a little over three years since I started and I am still the progress moving every month. This book will give you all the information to do the very same.

CHAPTER ONE: INTRODUCTION

BRIEF OVERVIEW OF THE COMMERCIAL CLEANING INDUSTRY

The commercial cleaning industry is a multifaceted sector dedicated to ensuring clean and sanitary environments across various businesses and institutions. Beyond traditional janitorial services, it encompasses a wide array of specialized cleaning tasks, including floor and carpet maintenance, window washing, and sanitation services tailored to meet the unique needs of diverse industries. The industry's significance lies not only in enhancing the aesthetic appeal of spaces but also in promoting employee well-being, productivity, and customer satisfaction. Characterized by adherence to regulations, the integration of cutting-edge cleaning technologies, and a competitive landscape, commercial cleaning responds to market demands and evolving public health concerns. The COVID-19 pandemic has underscored the industry's critical role, intensifying the focus on sanitation and hygiene. With a diverse clientele ranging from offices to healthcare facilities, the commercial cleaning sector offers opportunities for entrepreneurs to thrive by delivering quality services and staying abreast of industry trends.

IMPORTANCE OF CLEANLINESS FOR BUSINESSES

The importance of cleanliness for businesses cannot be overstated, as it directly influences various facets of their operations. A clean and well-maintained environment is crucial for creating a positive first impression on clients, customers, and visitors. Beyond aesthetics, cleanliness plays a pivotal role in fostering a healthy and useful workplace for employees. Regular and thorough cleaning not only reduces the risk of illnesses but also contributes to a conducive atmosphere for concentration and creativity. In sectors such as healthcare, hospitality, and food services, stringent cleanliness standards are imperative to ensure the well-being and safety of clients and customers.

Cleanliness is closely tied to the overall reputation and credibility of a business, influencing customer satisfaction and loyalty. In today's landscape, with heightened awareness of health and safety, businesses that prioritize cleanliness not only comply with regulations but also gain a competitive edge in the market.

Commercial cleaning businesses are essential because they provide specialized services that enable businesses to maintain impeccable standards of cleanliness. These professional services go beyond routine janitorial tasks, offering expertise in utilizing the right cleaning agents, equipment, and techniques for various industries and spaces. Commercial cleaning businesses play a crucial role in supporting other businesses by ensuring compliance with health and safety standards, creating a sanitary environment for employees and customers, and enhancing the overall image of the business. Their services are particularly invaluable in settings where cleanliness is paramount, such as hospitals, restaurants, offices, and educational institutions. Commercial cleaning businesses act as partners in the success of other enterprises, contributing to the overall health, productivity, and professionalism of the business environment.

MOTIVATION FOR STARTING A COMMERCIAL CLEANING BUSINESS

The personal motivation for starting a commercial cleaning business can stem from various factors that align with an individual's aspirations and values. For some entrepreneurs, the desire for autonomy and the opportunity to be their own boss can be a driving force. The prospect of building and managing a business independently, making decisions, and charting one's course can be highly motivating. Additionally, the commercial cleaning industry offers a relatively accessible entry point for individuals with a strong work ethic and a willingness to learn. The potential for financial independence and the ability to directly reap the rewards of hard work serve as powerful motivators, especially for those seeking a path to entrepreneurship.

Another personal motivation for starting a commercial cleaning business may be the tangible impact on the local community. Entrepreneurs in this industry contribute to creating cleaner, healthier, and more pleasant environments for businesses, institutions, and individuals. The sense of fulfillment that comes from knowing that the services provided positively impact the well-being and productivity of others can be a compelling motivator. Moreover, the personal satisfaction derived from building a business that aligns with eco-friendly practices or offers specialized cleaning solutions can add an additional layer of meaning to the entrepreneurial journey. Overall, personal motivation for entering the commercial cleaning business often involves a combination of a desire for independence, financial success, and the opportunity to make a positive difference in the communities served.

CHAPTER TWO: UNDERSTANDING THE INDUSTRY

MARKET RESEARCH AND ANALYSIS

Market research and analysis are pivotal steps in establishing and growing a successful commercial cleaning business. Thoroughly understanding the market landscape, identifying key opportunities, and assessing potential challenges lay the foundation for strategic decision-making. In this section, we delve into the essential aspects of market research and analysis for your commercial cleaning venture.

Before diving into the specifics, it's crucial to gain a general understanding of the commercial cleaning market. This involves analyzing the size, trends, and dynamics that shape the industry. Consider factors such as the overall demand for cleaning services, regional variations, and emerging trends within the commercial cleaning sector. This broad perspective forms the backdrop against which you'll tailor your business strategies.

The commercial cleaning industry serves a diverse range of sectors, each with its unique cleaning needs. Conduct market research to identify target industries and clients that align with your business goals. This may include offices, healthcare facilities, educational institutions, retail spaces, or industrial complexes. Analyze the cleaning requirements and regulations specific to each sector to tailor your services accordingly.

A comprehensive competitor analysis is essential for positioning your commercial cleaning business effectively. Identify key competitors in your target market and assess their strengths, weaknesses, and market share. Understand their service offerings, pricing strategies, and customer satisfaction levels. This analysis not only informs your competitive positioning but also highlights opportunities for differentiation and innovation.

A SWOT analysis (Strengths, Weaknesses, Opportunities, Threats) is a strategic tool that provides a detailed understanding of your business's internal and external factors. Evaluate your business's strengths, such as specialized services or a strong local presence and address potential weaknesses. Identify opportunities in the market, such as emerging trends or underserved niches, while mitigating potential threats, such as economic downturns or increased competition.

The commercial cleaning industry is subject to various regulations related to health, safety, and environmental standards. Stay abreast of local, state, and federal regulations that impact your business operations. Ensure that your services comply with industry standards and safety regulations. This not only avoids legal complications but also enhances your business's credibility in the eyes of clients.

Understanding your potential clients' needs and preferences is central to developing services that resonate with the market. Conduct surveys, interviews, or focus groups to gather insights into customer expectations, pain points, and priorities. This customer-centric approach informs the customization of your services, ensuring they align with the specific requirements of your target audience.

The commercial cleaning industry evolves with emerging technologies and changing customer expectations. Stay informed about market trends and innovations that could impact your business. This includes advancements in eco-friendly cleaning solutions, smart cleaning technologies, and industry-specific trends. Adapting to these trends positions your business as forward-thinking and responsive to market dynamics.

Economic conditions influence the demand for commercial cleaning services. Assess economic factors such as employment rates, business growth, and real estate trends in your target market. Understanding these factors helps anticipate fluctuations in demand and adjust your business strategies accordingly. Additionally, economic stability contributes to the overall viability and growth potential of your commercial cleaning venture.

Based on your market research findings, craft a unique value proposition that sets your commercial cleaning business apart. Emphasize key differentiators, whether it's specialized services, competitive pricing, or a commitment to sustainability. Your value proposition should resonate with the identified needs and preferences of your target audience, creating a compelling reason for clients to choose your services over competitors.

Market research is an ongoing process, not a one-time activity. Regularly revisit and update your research to stay attuned to market changes, customer preferences, and emerging trends. This iterative approach ensures that your commercial cleaning business remains agile and responsive in a dynamic industry.

Much can be gained by thorough market research and analysis form the bedrock of a successful commercial cleaning business. Understanding the market dynamics, identifying target clients, analyzing competitors, and staying abreast of industry trends, you position your business for strategic growth and sustainable success.

LEGAL CONSIDERATIONS

Establishing and operating a commercial cleaning business comes with a set of legal considerations that demand attention and diligence. From compliance with regulations to safeguarding contracts, this chapter explores the legal landscape and provides insights into ensuring your commercial cleaning business operates within legal parameters.

Choosing the right business structure is a crucial legal consideration. Options include sole proprietorship, partnership, limited liability company (LLC), or corporation. Each structure has distinct legal implications, affecting factors such as personal liability, taxation, and regulatory requirements. Register your business with the appropriate authorities, obtaining the necessary licenses and permits to operate legally.

The commercial cleaning industry is subject to health and safety regulations aimed at protecting workers and clients. Comply with Occupational Safety and Health Administration (OSHA) standards, providing proper training, safety equipment, and protocols for cleaning staff. Regularly review and update safety measures to align with industry best practices and regulatory changes.

Given the impact of cleaning operations on the environment, environmental compliance is a key consideration. Adhere to regulations related to waste disposal, chemical usage, and sustainability practices. Implement eco-friendly cleaning solutions and procedures to align with environmental standards and contribute to the growing demand for sustainable business practices.

Clear and legally sound contracts are essential for protecting your commercial cleaning business. Develop comprehensive service agreements that outline terms, scope of services, payment terms, and liability provisions. Address issues such as insurance coverage and indemnification to protect your business in case of disputes or accidents. Consulting with a legal professional to draft and review contracts ensures legal clarity and protection.

Navigating employment laws is critical for maintaining a compliant and fair workplace. Understand wage and hour laws, employee classification (e.g., full-time, part-time, independent contractors), and workplace safety requirements. Establish clear employment policies, including those related to harassment, discrimination, and termination procedures. Regularly update policies to align with evolving employment laws.

Insurance is a fundamental aspect of risk management for a commercial cleaning business. Obtain adequate insurance coverage to protect against liabilities such as property damage, injuries, and accidents. Consider general liability insurance, workers' compensation insurance, and commercial property insurance to provide comprehensive coverage for potential risks. Regularly review and update insurance policies to ensure continued protection. I would suggest considering Hiscox Business insurance.

Adhering to tax regulations is paramount for the financial health of your commercial cleaning business. Understand federal, state, and local tax obligations, including income taxes, sales taxes, and payroll taxes. Keep meticulous financial records, consult with a tax professional for guidance, and file taxes accurately and on time to avoid legal repercussions. Another suggestion I would make is to try a company named Homebase for all of your payroll needs.

Protecting your brand and intellectual property is crucial in the competitive commercial cleaning industry. Trademark your business name, logo, and any unique services or products to prevent unauthorized use by competitors. Regularly monitor and enforce your intellectual property rights to safeguard your brand identity.

In an increasingly digital world, data protection and privacy considerations are paramount. Safeguard client information, employee records, and any other sensitive data collected during your operations. Implement cybersecurity measures, comply with data protection regulations, and communicate transparently with clients about your data handling practices.

Despite proactive measures, disputes may arise. Establish clear dispute resolution procedures in contracts and consider alternative dispute resolution methods such as mediation or arbitration. Cultivate a relationship with a legal professional experienced in business law to provide ongoing legal advice, ensuring that your commercial cleaning business remains informed and compliant with evolving legal requirements.

Navigating the legal considerations of a commercial cleaning business requires a proactive and informed approach. By understanding and adhering to business structure requirements, safety regulations, contractual obligations, and other legal facets, you lay the legal foundations for a resilient and compliant enterprise. Regularly reassessing legal considerations ensures that your business adapts to changes in the legal landscape and operates with integrity and legality.

CHAPTER THREE: CRAFTING A GOOD BUSINESS PLAN

Crafting a good business plan is not just a procedural step in launching a commercial cleaning business; it is a fundamental and indispensable process that lays the groundwork for success. This chapter explores the critical reasons why aspiring entrepreneurs in the commercial cleaning industry must invest time and effort in creating a detailed and well-thought-out business plan.

STRATEGIC ROADMAP

A business plan serves as a strategic roadmap, providing a clear direction for the commercial cleaning business. It outlines the mission, vision, and objectives, acting as a compass that guides decision-making and goal setting. By defining the business's purpose and desired outcomes, entrepreneurs can align their efforts and resources effectively, fostering a cohesive and purpose-driven venture.

For those seeking external funding or partnerships, a well-crafted business plan is essential for attracting investors and stakeholders. Whether approaching banks, lenders, or potential business partners, a comprehensive plan demonstrates diligence, foresight, and a thorough understanding of the commercial cleaning market. Investors are more likely to support a venture that has a well-defined strategy, clear financial projections, and a solid plan for mitigating risks.

OPERATIONAL CLARITY

A business plan provides operational clarity by detailing the day-to-day processes, staffing requirements, and quality control measures of the commercial cleaning business. This clarity is crucial for maintaining consistency in service delivery, ensuring that employees understand their roles, and establishing efficient workflows. Operational clarity enhances the overall efficiency of the business, contributing to client satisfaction and long-term success.

FINANCIAL MANAGEMENT

Effective financial management is a linchpin of business success, and a well-structured business plan is a key tool in this regard. It includes detailed financial projections, budgets, and a break-even analysis, offering insights into the financial health and sustainability of the commercial cleaning business. Entrepreneurs can make informed decisions about pricing, expenditures, and investment strategies, optimizing financial resources for maximum impact.

RISK MITIGATION

Every business venture carries inherent risks, and a business plan serves as a preemptive tool for risk mitigation. By conducting a SWOT analysis (Strengths, Weaknesses, Opportunities, Threats), entrepreneurs can identify potential challenges and develop contingency plans. This proactive approach helps in navigating uncertainties and adapting to unforeseen circumstances, enhancing the resilience of the commercial cleaning business.

MARKET UNDERSTANDING

In the dynamic landscape of the commercial cleaning industry, a business plan demonstrates a deep understanding of the market. It includes thorough market research, competitor analysis, and insights into target audiences. This knowledge empowers entrepreneurs to make informed strategic decisions, adapt to changing market conditions, and capitalize on emerging opportunities.

GOAL MEASUREMENT AND ADAPTABILITY

A business plan establishes measurable goals and timelines, enabling entrepreneurs to track progress and success. Regular reviews of the plan facilitate adaptability, allowing the commercial cleaning business to pivot when necessary. Whether it's responding to shifts in market trends or adjusting operational strategies, the business plan acts as a living document that evolves with the business.

COMMUNICATION TOOL

Internally and externally, a business plan serves as a communication tool. Within the business, it aligns team members with overarching vision and goals. Externally, it communicates the business's value proposition, differentiation strategies, and potential for growth. A well-articulated plan can also be used to attract clients, as it instills confidence in the professionalism and reliability of the commercial cleaning services offered.

In essence, crafting a good business plan for a commercial cleaning business is not just a formality—it is an essential and strategic exercise that positions the venture for success. From attracting investors to guiding day-to-day operations, the business plan is a multifaceted tool that empowers entrepreneurs to navigate challenges, seize opportunities, and build a resilient and thriving enterprise.

BELOW IS THE OUTLINE OF THE BUSINESS PLAN I USED FOR MY BUSINESS.

Name of the Company:

Website Address:

Email Address:

Phone:

What is the name of your product/ service and how does it work?
What industry does your business belong?
What are the names of the people involved in the business and what are the positions they hold?
Tell me four main city your business is targeting:
What is the reason behind you starting your business?
What is your vision statement? Bring luxury quality in every product at a low cost?
Where are you located your business address?
What or who is the competition in your industry?
What is your business objective?
Who are your target markets?
If using a website describe your commerce platform and also send us your website address
What is the level of experience you have in this industry?

Provide a short biography leading up to the point you started the company.

What are the costs of the monthly expenses you expect to incur?

Monthly expenses:

Rent:

Phone:

Website:

Advertising:

Office Supply:

Insurance:

Are they any assets or liabilities that you are presently carrying?

When and what are the steps you plan to take to make your business a success?

Section 2 (Financial Analysis)

How much net profit are you anticipating to make in your first, second, third, fourth and fifth years?

Kindly list some expenses you will incur in the course of operation. Indicate each expense with price if it is a monthly or yearly expense.

At what rate would you be offering your services and at what profit margin?

How many staff members do you have?

Any form of loan or investment?

Owner investment or shareholder contribution?

Fill the start-up table below. Requirements: Need an advertisement plan, market plan, monetary certification, lbt license, advertisements .. Start-up expenses

Legal stationery:

Insurance:

Rent:

Computer:

Total start-up expenses:

CHAPTER FOUR: SETTING UP YOUR OPERATION

NECESSARY EQUIPMENT AND SUPPLIES

A successful commercial cleaning business relies heavily on having the necessary equipment and supplies to deliver high-quality services efficiently. Essential equipment includes industrial-grade Dyson vacuum cleaners, floor buffers, carpet cleaning machines, power washers, and window cleaning tools. The choice of cleaning supplies is equally crucial, encompassing a range of environmentally friendly and effective cleaning agents, disinfectants, sanitizers, and specialized solutions for various surfaces. My personal favorites are Barkeeper Friend Cleaner and Dove soap.

Additionally, the business should invest in quality microfiber cloths, mops, and durable cleaning tools to ensure thorough and hygienic cleaning processes. Safety gear such as gloves, masks, and protective eyewear is imperative for the well-being of cleaning staff. Regular maintenance and timely replacement of equipment and supplies are essential to uphold service standards and meet client expectations. By investing in the right tools and products, a commercial cleaning business can not only enhance its operational efficiency but also establish a reputation for delivering exceptional cleanliness and hygiene to its clients.

BAR
KEEPERS
FRIEND
CLEANSER
STREAM DAMAGE
DAWN
PLATINUM
REMOVE 99%

STAFFING REQUIREMENTS

Staffing is a critical aspect of a successful commercial cleaning business, as the quality of services often depends on the expertise and dedication of the cleaning team. The staffing requirements encompass hiring skilled and reliable cleaners who are trained in various cleaning techniques and safety protocols. Recruitment efforts should prioritize individuals with attention to detail, reliability, and a strong work ethic. Training programs should be implemented to ensure that the cleaning staff is well-versed in the use of specialized equipment and eco-friendly cleaning practices. Establishing a positive team culture is essential for fostering collaboration and motivation among staff members. Adequate staffing levels are necessary to meet client demands, especially during peak cleaning times or when taking on larger projects. Additionally, effective communication channels should be in place to address any issues promptly and ensure a smooth workflow. By investing in a competent and well-trained cleaning team, a commercial cleaning business can build a reputation for professionalism and consistently deliver high-quality services to its clients.

ESTABLISHING EFFICIENT CLEANING PROCESSES

Establishing efficient cleaning processes is fundamental for the success and effectiveness of a commercial cleaning business. The development of systematic and well-defined procedures ensures consistency in service delivery, enhances productivity, and contributes to overall client satisfaction. The first step involves assessing the specific cleaning needs of clients and tailoring processes accordingly. Creating a detailed cleaning checklist for each job, outlining tasks and frequency, helps in maintaining organization and accountability. Efficient scheduling and time management are crucial elements, optimizing the use of resources and minimizing downtime.

Additionally, implementing quality control measures, such as regular inspections and client feedback systems, ensures that cleaning standards remain consistently high. Investing in training programs for cleaning staff on the latest cleaning techniques and equipment promotes proficiency and adaptability. By continuously refining and optimizing cleaning processes, a commercial cleaning business can differentiate itself in the market, build a strong reputation for reliability, and foster long-term client relationships.

CHAPTER FIVE: MARKETING AND BRANDING

In the competitive landscape of the commercial cleaning industry, effective marketing and branding are pivotal for establishing a strong presence, attracting clients, and differentiating your business. This chapter explores the essential elements and strategies to elevate the marketing and branding efforts of your commercial cleaning business.

CRAFTING A STRONG BRAND IDENTITY

A compelling brand identity is the cornerstone of successful marketing. Develop a memorable logo, tagline, and visual elements that convey professionalism, reliability, and a commitment to cleanliness. In the very beginning I wore scrubs that had my logo on it. This gave me a professional appearance and instant branding. Consistency in branding across all platforms fosters brand recognition and reinforces your business's values in the eyes of potential clients.

ESTABLISHING AN ONLINE PRESENCE

In today's digital age, having a robust online presence is non-negotiable. Create a professional website that showcases your services, highlights client testimonials, and provides easy contact options. Leverage social media platforms to engage with your audience, share valuable content, and build a community around your brand. Utilize online advertising and search engine optimization (SEO) to enhance visibility in online searches.

TARGETED MARKETING CAMPAIGNS

Tailor your marketing efforts to reach your target audience effectively. So, you may wonder, "How do I get more clients?" First, identify key demographics and industries that align with your services and develop targeted marketing campaigns. In order to start growing your business, you must do great quality work so they can refer you to others. Understand, it's not going to happen overnight. I started out bad and ended up as a great cleaner and entrepreneur so if I can do it, you can do it as well. Pass out business cards or door hangers by using the door-to-door method or go into business offices, medical offices, hospitals, restaurants, apartment complexes and any other place you can think of that could need your help. Also do cold emailing and cold calling. I used to do 5-20 cold calls per week and my cold call script was like this…

"Hello, my name is Shanaya Pearson I am owner of cleaning company I was wondering can I speak to manager?"

"Manager is speaking," they would often reply.

"Ok, I was calling to see if you need any cleaning at your facility. I'm an owner of cleaning company."

"Yes," they would say. "Can you come for walk through?"

"Sure," I would say. "What day?"

After that I would go in for a walkthrough and give them a quote.

BUILDING A CONTENT STRATEGY

Content is a powerful tool for demonstrating expertise and building trust. Develop a content strategy that includes blog posts, articles, infographics, and videos related to the commercial cleaning industry. Address common challenges, provide cleaning tips, and showcase your knowledge. This not only positions your business as an authority but also improves your search engine rankings.

CLIENT TESTIMONIALS AND CASE STUDIES

Positive reviews and testimonials from satisfied clients are invaluable marketing assets. Encourage clients to provide feedback and share their positive experiences. Consider creating case studies that highlight specific challenges your business addressed and the successful outcomes.

Authentic stories from happy clients can be compelling marketing tools that instill confidence in potential customers.

NETWORKING AND COMMUNITY ENGAGEMENT

Building relationships within the local community is a potent marketing strategy. Attend local business events, join industry associations, and participate in community initiatives. Networking not only raises awareness of your business but also opens doors to potential collaborations and referrals. Establishing your commercial cleaning business as an active and engaged community member fosters trust and credibility.

OFFERING VALUE-ADDED SERVICES

Differentiate your business by offering value-added services that go beyond basic cleaning. This could include eco-friendly cleaning options, specialized disinfection services, or innovative cleaning technologies. Highlight these unique offerings in your marketing materials to attract clients who prioritize sustainability and advanced cleaning solutions.

IMPLEMENTING REFERRAL PROGRAMS

Word of mouth is a potent marketing tool. Implement referral programs that incentivize current clients and partners to refer your services to others. Consider offering discounts, free services, or other perks for successful referrals. A well-designed referral program can expand your client base and enhance your business's reputation.

MEASURING AND ANALYZING RESULTS

Regularly measure the effectiveness of your marketing efforts. Utilize analytics tools to track website traffic, social media engagement, and lead generation. Analyze which strategies are delivering the best results and adjust your marketing plan accordingly. A data-driven approach ensures that your marketing efforts are strategic and impactful.

CHAPTER SIX: CRISIS MANAGEMENT AND REPUTATION

In the dynamic landscape of the commercial cleaning industry, unforeseen challenges and crises may arise, posing threats to your business's reputation. How you navigate and manage these crises can significantly impact the trust and confidence of clients. This chapter delves into the importance of crisis management, strategies for proactive reputation protection, and effective communication during challenging times.

Crisis management begins with proactive planning. Anticipate potential crises that could affect your commercial cleaning business, whether they involve accidents, negative publicity, or operational disruptions. Develop a comprehensive crisis management plan that outlines response strategies, communication protocols, and designated responsibilities within your team. Regularly review and update this plan to ensure its relevance in evolving circumstances.

Open and transparent communication is paramount during a crisis. Establish communication channels that facilitate swift and accurate dissemination of information to your clients, employees, and stakeholders. Be proactive in addressing concerns, providing regular updates, and offering solutions. Transparency fosters trust and demonstrates your commitment to addressing challenges with integrity.

In the event of a crisis, prioritize addressing client concerns promptly and professionally. Establish clear channels for clients to voice their concerns and complaints. Responding swiftly and empathetically to client feedback demonstrates a commitment to customer satisfaction and can mitigate potential damage to your business's reputation.

In the age of social media, crises can quickly escalate online. Implement robust social media monitoring to track mentions, comments, and discussions related to your commercial cleaning business. Respond thoughtfully to negative comments, addressing concerns publicly when appropriate and redirecting conversations to private channels for resolution. Social media can be a powerful tool for managing and repairing your reputation.

Your staff is a crucial component in crisis management. Train employees in crisis response protocols, ensuring they understand their roles and responsibilities. Foster a culture of preparedness and responsiveness among your team. Equip them with the skills to handle client concerns, manage communication effectively, and contribute to the resolution of crises.

Proactively engage in positive public relations efforts to build a reservoir of goodwill. Highlight your commercial cleaning business's community involvement, sustainability initiatives, and positive client testimonials. A positive public image established during ordinary times can serve as a protective buffer during a crisis, influencing how your business is perceived by clients and the public.

Regularly monitor your business's online reputation through reviews, ratings, and feedback platforms. Address negative reviews promptly and professionally, demonstrating a commitment to resolving issues. Actively manage your online presence by showcasing positive aspects of your business, sharing success stories, and maintaining an active and positive engagement with your audience.

Every crisis provides an opportunity for learning and adaptation. Conduct post-crisis evaluations to assess the effectiveness of your response strategies. Identify areas for improvement and implement changes to strengthen your crisis management plan. Learning from past experiences ensures that your commercial cleaning business becomes more resilient and better prepared for future challenges.

Navigating legal considerations is crucial in crisis management. Consult with legal professionals to ensure that your crisis response strategies align with legal requirements. Address any potential liability concerns and adhere to regulations related to communication, privacy, and client protection during crises.

Once a crisis has been managed, focus on rebuilding trust and moving forward. Communicate transparently about the steps taken to address the situation, implement improvements, and prevent similar issues in the future. Showcase your commitment to learning and growth, reinforcing the positive aspects of your commercial cleaning business to rebuild and strengthen relationships with clients and stakeholders.

Crisis management and reputation protection are integral components of sustaining a successful commercial cleaning business. By proactively planning for crises, communicating transparently, and learning from challenges, you not only protect your business's reputation but also position it for long-term resilience and success in a competitive industry.

CHAPTER SEVEN: NAVIGATING CHALLANGES

Running a commercial cleaning business is not without its challenges. From dealing with competition to managing client expectations, this chapter explores the common hurdles faced by entrepreneurs in the commercial cleaning industry and provides strategies for navigating these challenges effectively.

INTENSE COMPETITION

The commercial cleaning industry is highly competitive, with numerous businesses vying for clients. To navigate this challenge, focus on differentiating your services. Highlight your unique selling propositions, whether it's specialized cleaning services, eco-friendly practices, or exceptional customer service. Develop a strategic marketing plan that emphasizes what sets your business apart and consistently delivers on those promises to build a competitive edge.

STAFFING CHALLENGES

Finding and retaining reliable cleaning staff can be a persistent challenge. Implement robust recruitment and training programs to attract skilled and motivated employees. Foster a positive work culture that encourages employee satisfaction and loyalty. Regularly communicate with your staff to understand their needs and concerns, addressing any issues promptly. Providing competitive wages and benefits can also contribute to employee retention.

CLIENT EXPECTATIONS AND SATISFACTION

Meeting and exceeding client expectations is critical for retaining business in the commercial cleaning industry. Clearly communicate service offerings, pricing structures, and expectations from the outset. Implement rigorous quality control measures to ensure consistent service delivery. Regularly seek client feedback and address any concerns proactively. Establishing open lines of communication with clients fosters trust and contributes to long-term satisfaction.

PRICING PRESSURES

Clients may exert pressure on pricing, especially in competitive markets. Conduct a thorough analysis of your costs to determine fair and competitive pricing. Emphasize the value-added services your business provides and communicate the benefits of choosing your services over lower-priced alternatives. Consider flexible pricing structures and explore cost-saving measures without compromising the quality of your services.

CHANGING REGULATIONS AND
COMPLIANCE

The commercial cleaning industry is subject to various regulations, including health and safety standards and environmental compliance. Stay informed about changes in regulations and ensure that your business is fully compliant. Develop robust safety protocols and provide ongoing training to staff to adhere to industry standards. Proactive compliance measures not only mitigate risks but also enhance the credibility of your business.

TECHNOLOGY INTEGRATION CHALLENGES

Adopting and integrating technology into cleaning processes can pose challenges for some businesses. Invest in user-friendly software solutions that enhance operational efficiency. Provide adequate training for staff to adapt to new technologies. Explore innovative cleaning equipment and solutions that improve the quality and speed of your services. Embracing technology can be a transformative step in overcoming operational challenges.

SEASONAL FLUCTUATIONS

Commercial cleaning businesses may experience seasonal fluctuations in demand. Develop strategies to address these variations, such as offering specialized seasonal services or diversifying into industries with steadier demand. Implement effective scheduling and staff management practices to adapt to peak and off-peak periods, ensuring optimal resource utilization throughout the year.

MANAGING CASH FLOW

Cash flow management is crucial for the financial health of any business. Develop robust invoicing and payment systems to ensure timely receipt of payments. Negotiate favorable payment terms with suppliers to optimize cash flow. Monitor expenses closely and create contingency plans for unforeseen financial challenges. A proactive approach to financial management helps maintain stability during fluctuations.

TECHNOLOGICAL DISRUPTIONS

The commercial cleaning industry is witnessing technological advancements that may disrupt traditional business models. Stay informed about emerging technologies and trends in the industry. Consider adopting innovations that enhance efficiency and sustainability. Proactively adapting to technological changes positions your business as forward-thinking and resilient in the face of industry evolution.

CRISIS MANAGEMENT AND REPUTATION

Unforeseen crises, such as public relations challenges or client complaints, can pose significant threats to a commercial cleaning business. Develop a crisis management plan that includes transparent communication, swift resolution of issues, and a commitment to client satisfaction. Protect and enhance your reputation by actively managing online reviews and maintaining open communication channels with clients.

Navigating the challenges of a commercial cleaning business requires a combination of strategic planning, adaptability, and a commitment to continuous improvement. By addressing these challenges proactively and implementing effective solutions, your business can weather uncertainties and emerge stronger in the dynamic commercial cleaning industry.

CHAPTER EIGHT: SCALING YOUR BUSINESS

As your commercial cleaning business gains traction and success, the next logical step is scaling to achieve even greater heights. This chapter explores key strategies and considerations for scaling your operations, expanding your client base, and solidifying your position in the market.

STREAMLINING OPERATIONS FOR EFFICIENCY

Before embarking on the scaling journey, ensure that your operations are streamlined and efficient. Review and optimize your cleaning processes, staffing structures, and quality control measures. Implement technologies and systems that enhance productivity and minimize operational bottlenecks. An efficient foundation is essential for managing increased workloads effectively.

EXPANDING SERVICE OFFERINGS

Diversifying your service offerings is a strategic way to attract a broader clientele and increase revenue streams. Consider introducing specialized cleaning services, such as post-construction cleanup, carpet cleaning, or industrial cleaning. Expanding your range of services not only meets diverse client needs but also positions your business as a comprehensive solution provider in the commercial cleaning industry.

GEOGRAPHIC EXPANSION

Scaling often involves reaching new markets and expanding your geographic footprint. Evaluate neighboring areas or regions with untapped potential. Conduct thorough market research to understand local needs and competition. Establishing satellite offices or partnering with local businesses can facilitate a smooth expansion into new territories.

FRANCHISING OPPORTUNITIES

Franchising is a powerful strategy for rapid scaling. It allows entrepreneurs to replicate the success of their business model in different locations while benefiting from the strength of the established brand. Before franchising, ensure that your operations, branding, and support systems are well-documented and easily replicable. Develop comprehensive franchise agreements and support structures to maintain consistency across franchises.

STRATEGIC PARTNERSHIPS AND COLLABORATIONS

Collaborating with other businesses or forming strategic partnerships can be a mutually beneficial way to scale. Consider partnerships with property management companies, real estate agents, or facility management firms to access a broader client base. Joint ventures and collaborations can provide access to new opportunities, clients, and resources.

INVESTING IN MARKETING AND DIGITAL PRESENCE

Scaling requires an amplified marketing effort to increase brand visibility. Invest in targeted marketing campaigns, both online and offline. Utilize digital marketing strategies such as search engine optimization (SEO), online advertising, and social media marketing to reach a wider audience. A strong digital presence enhances credibility and attracts clients in the digital age.

LEVERAGING TECHNOLOGY FOR EFFICIENCY

Embrace technology to enhance efficiency and scalability. Implement software solutions for scheduling, invoicing, and customer relationship management. Explore the use of specialized cleaning equipment and emerging technologies that improve the quality and speed of your services. Technology integration streamlines operations and supports the scalability of your commercial cleaning business.

EMPLOYEE TRAINING AND DEVELOPMENT

As your business grows, investing in employee training and development becomes imperative. Ensure that your staff is equipped with the necessary skills to meet increased demand and adhere to high-quality standards. Implement training programs that align with industry best practices and emerging trends in the commercial cleaning sector.

FINANCIAL PLANNING AND CAPITAL ALLOCATION

Successful scaling requires careful financial planning. Allocate capital strategically to support expansion initiatives, whether it's hiring additional staff, investing in marketing, or opening new locations. Consider securing additional funding if necessary and ensure that your financial infrastructure can support the increased demands of a scaled-up business.

QUALITY CONTROL AND CUSTOMER SATISFACTION

Maintain a relentless focus on quality control and customer satisfaction throughout the scaling process. Consistency in service delivery is crucial for preserving the reputation of your business. Implement robust quality control measures, seek client feedback regularly, and address any issues promptly to ensure that the quality of your services remains unwavering.

Scaling your commercial cleaning business is a multifaceted endeavor that requires strategic planning, operational efficiency, and a commitment to maintaining the quality that defines your brand. By carefully navigating these strategies, your business can not only expand its reach but also solidify its position as a leader in the competitive commercial cleaning industry.

CHAPTER NINE: SUSTAINABILITY AND ENVIORMENTAL PRACTICES

As global awareness of environmental issues rises, businesses are increasingly expected to adopt sustainable and eco-friendly practices. This chapter explores the importance of sustainability in the commercial cleaning industry and provides insights into implementing environmental practices that benefit both the planet and your business.

The commercial cleaning industry has a significant impact on the environment due to the use of cleaning chemicals, disposable products, and energy-intensive equipment. Acknowledging this impact is the first step toward implementing sustainability practices. The shift toward eco-friendly solutions not only benefits the environment but also aligns your business with the growing demand for socially responsible practices.

Replace conventional cleaning products with eco-friendly alternatives that are biodegradable, non-toxic, and derived from sustainable sources. Green cleaning products reduce the environmental impact of cleaning processes, improve indoor air quality, and contribute to a healthier work environment for both clients and cleaning staff. Communicate the switch to eco-friendly products in your marketing materials to attract environmentally conscious clients.

Upgrade cleaning equipment to energy-efficient models that consume less power and water. High-efficiency vacuum cleaners (I highly recommend Dyson vacuum cleaners), steam cleaners, and other tools reduce energy consumption while maintaining or improving cleaning effectiveness. Additionally, consider implementing cleaning schedules that optimize energy usage, such as cleaning during off-peak hours or using natural daylight whenever possible.

Implement water conservation measures in your cleaning processes. Encourage staff to use water judiciously and fix any leaks promptly. Explore cleaning methods that minimize water usage, such as microfiber mops that require less water for effective cleaning. Communicate your commitment to water conservation in marketing materials to appeal to environmentally conscious clients.

Minimize waste generation by adopting practices that reduce, reuse, and recycle. Invest in reusable cleaning cloths and mop heads instead of disposable alternatives. Implement waste sorting programs to recycle materials like paper, plastic, and cardboard. Communicate your waste reduction initiatives to clients, showcasing your commitment to minimizing the environmental footprint of your cleaning operations.

Choose suppliers that prioritize sustainable packaging for cleaning products and supplies. Opt for packaging made from recycled materials or materials that are easily recyclable. Communicate your preference for sustainable packaging to suppliers to encourage eco-friendly practices throughout the supply chain. This not only aligns with your sustainability goals but also sets expectations for suppliers to adopt environmentally responsible practices.

Educate your cleaning staff on the importance of sustainability and provide training on eco-friendly cleaning practices. Foster a culture of environmental responsibility by encouraging staff to adopt sustainable habits both at work and in their personal lives. Engaged and knowledgeable staff play a crucial role in successfully implementing and maintaining sustainability practices.

Consider obtaining certifications and eco-labels that validate your commitment to sustainability. Certifications from recognized organizations, such as the Green Seal or EcoLogo, provide credibility and assurance to clients that your business adheres to stringent environmental standards. Displaying these certifications in your marketing materials can attract clients seeking environmentally responsible cleaning services.

Proactively seek out and collaborate with clients and other cleaning businesses who share your commitment to sustainability. Position your business as a partner in their environmental initiatives, offering tailored solutions that align with their green goals. Collaborating with eco-conscious clients not only enhances your business's reputation but also creates a mutually beneficial relationship based on shared values.

Sustainability is an evolving field, and new practices and technologies emerge regularly. Commit to continuous improvement by staying informed about the latest developments in sustainable cleaning practices. Be adaptable and willing to incorporate new eco-friendly solutions into your operations. Demonstrating a commitment to ongoing sustainability efforts positions your business as a leader in environmentally responsible cleaning practices.

Embracing sustainability in your commercial cleaning business not only contributes to a healthier planet but also enhances your business's reputation and attracts clients who prioritize environmentally conscious services. By integrating eco-friendly practices into your operations, you position your business as a responsible steward of the environment while staying ahead of industry trends.

CHAPTER TEN: CONCLUSION

In conclusion, aspiring commercial cleaning entrepreneurs should approach the industry with enthusiasm, recognizing the diverse opportunities and the critical role they play in promoting cleanliness and well-being. Crafting a comprehensive business plan, understanding market dynamics, and embracing innovative and sustainable practices are key steps in establishing a successful venture. The importance of efficient processes, strategic marketing, and a customer-centric approach cannot be overstated. Moreover, navigating competition, handling client feedback constructively, and exploring expansion possibilities contribute to long-term success. By prioritizing professionalism, quality service, and sustainability, aspiring entrepreneurs can carve a niche in the competitive commercial cleaning landscape. The journey may present challenges, but each obstacle is an opportunity for growth. With dedication, adaptability, and a commitment to excellence, entrepreneurs can not only build a thriving commercial cleaning business but also make a positive impact on the businesses and communities they serve. The future holds promise for those who embark on this journey with passion and a vision for success.

CONTACT INFO

www.catresespecialservicesinc.com

(305) 481-7705

www.ingramcontent.com/pod-product-compliance
Lightning Source LLC
Chambersburg PA
CBHW061706130726
47996CB00006B/2177